What Are You After?

What Are You After?

Josephine Corcoran

Nine
Arches
Press

What Are You After?
Josephine Corcoran

ISBN: 978-1911027423

Cover artwork: 'Transience II' © Mary Petrovska
Instagram: @marypetrovskaartist

First published June 2018 by:

Nine Arches Press
Unit 14,
Sir Frank Whittle Business Centre,
Great Central Way, Rugby.
CV21 3XH
United Kingdom

www.ninearchespress.com

Printed in the United Kingdom by:
Imprint Digital

Nine Arches Press is supported using public funding by Arts Council England.

Supported using public funding by
ARTS COUNCIL
ENGLAND

CONTENTS

for Andrew, Kitty and Johnny

Honeymoon

I wouldn't call it a honeymoon,
those muffled nights in mothballed rooms.
With cake in the boot we pilgrimmed north,
taking a young marriage to old widows,

my father's brothers dead,
their crucifixes still hanging. In each house
we were given the double bed,
my aunties inviting us to fornicate

on concave mattresses, dead men's
seed. Had we come one week before,
you would have been given nothing
but dusty blankets on a downstairs floor.

I would have sunk, alone and deep,
into the mildewed sponge of a cousin's bed.
My aunties would have spread
as wide as angels in their marital sheets,

their doors ajar, the solemn whispers
of their night-time prayers beating
as sweet as deathbed love-making.
But our wedding vows were said,

so we sipped tea on upright chairs
still dimpled from Brylcreemed heads,
and rolled like screws in sideways jars
on shelves in locked-up sheds.

                              Seven years,
one son, one daughter later,
Jesus has been sent to us.
The aunts are gone, their houses stripped.
His legs are broken. Long marriages

thrown into landfill, and we laugh
when our little children ask
about our honeymoon. I see you dreaming
down our garden path, the broken body

in your hands. You are picturing
the twist of wire you'll use to bind his legs;
the nail, the hammer, the spirit level, the pencil
mark, the place he'll eternally outstare us.

I love the way our daughter sings
as her finger traces our wedding rings.

Dream while losing twins

My Dad has cycled from his forties
to see me, scraps of autumn debris
in his long black hair, although it's summer
and he was almost seventy when he died.

Naturally, he disturbs the settled classroom
but these are my favourite students
who return to their dictionaries as he lifts
a Bakelite telephone from my desk.

There is no wheelchair in this dream
so he leans on my students' heads
and necks and shoulders to drag
and hoist and slump himself into a seat.

I speak an unknown language.
My students, here to learn English,
are delighted. My father seems
to fill the room with confidence.

He makes a performance of untangling
the spiralled cord, dials combinations
of numbers, rustles through old receipts.
"Hello? *Hello?*" I signal to him

but of course he carries on.
There are hours of garbled speaking
then he re-arranges the cradle
and receiver on my desk.

"I can't get through."
I watch him move away,
turn to smile at me
through a square of glass.

It's not like leaving the cinema
when people exchange the dark
for sunlight; it's just me awake, bleeding,
in a room sweet with energy.

Supermoon, September 2014

The twins who left us waited
        thirteen years for me to see them

        as if I

never twisted like a pepper grinder
        or held the liver of them in my hands.

They appear as easily as footballs
        thrown over next door's hedge,

the sky has given up its hope
        of holding onto them.

        And you and I

stand close as lovers in a gallery,
        the window framing an empty night,

our interlocking fingers full
        of all that we withhold

        from one another.

You say it's a bomber's moon,
        gardens lit up like tablecloths,

owls calling the unlived lives
        of rabbits and mice.

        What if tonight

blue-washed beaches
        spill over with teenagers,

their parents nowhere to be seen
        as they swim in the high tide.

Esther and Ezekiel

When it came to Confirmation my girl and boy
chose Old Testament names with matching letters

as if they knew that in their toddler days
they were mistaken for twins.

Those of us who believe in the Holy Spirit
forgive our children for receiving the sacrament

under false pretences, for pocketing gifts.
Faith is a long journey, our Priest says.

I offer up my doubts and, like Esther,
never mention God or miscarriage

in ordinary life. Nor do I talk about
Samuel L. Jackson when asked why

my son chose that name. This time
prayers have outlived violence.

He knows the lines by heart, as sure
as Tarantino of their provenance:

Blessed is he who, in the name of charity and good will,
Shepherds the weak through the valley of the darkness.

For he is truly his brother's keeper
And the finder of lost children.

Mis/Carriage

to miss   to not reach   to not get   to not have   to fail
to know others have not failed   to not win   to not be to
not know   to lose   to almost have to imagine, then lose
to never know   to always know you haven't   to always
never have not quite   to not keep   to not own   to not
possess   to come close, then fail   to cause hope to rise
and fall   to be the cause of disappointment   to bring
about and cause to fade applause   to be pitied   to be
given to and stolen from   to hear laughter swallowed
to be hope as it leaves   to let slip   to watch fall   to be
the falling   to dream you have/you are/ you did/you are
doing   to lose over and over again in dreams   to hold
again in dreams   to be lost   to know what you haven't
to feel brushed against the lightest touch   happiness perhaps
not never was to hold and not   to not arrive   to long for

carriage is fairytale   is fragile   is made of glass   is made
of pumpkin   is brought to life   is made   is godmother
made   is manufactured   is fashioned   is dreamed
about   is drawn up   is horse-drawn   is at midnight
is awaiting   is climbed into   is stepped inside   is fallen
asleep in   is rocking   is moonlight-filled   is speeding
with precious cargo inside   is rushing to meet   is gazed
from   gazed into

A dream while pregnant

I found a broodmare
fallen behind cushions,
unwakeable and slippery,
small enough to fill a padded envelope.
Holding her was like scooping well-set jelly.
I posted her to my doctor.

On the morning of that dream
a broodmare stared at me from a field,
saw my unborn daughter.
I watched the sharp hooves of her foal moving
like someone trapped behind a rubber curtain.

Nowadays, insomnia locks me inside
the algebra of dreams.
I puzzle over the broodmare;
my face and shape
appearing in her head;
if she arrived safely.

What are you after?

The Irish Potato Famine
A boat ticket to Liverpool
A green-fingered great-grandfather
A landscape gardening business
A shoebox of black and white photographs
Something I won't find anywhere else

A German seaman who abandoned his family
A seaside town in the North West of England
A new wife with a Scottish surname
English-speaking children
Three baker's shops
Blond hair and blue eyes strong in the gene pool
Something for my children

An apprentice gas-fitter nicknamed 'Paddy'
His trousers pulled down, his balls painted green
A teenaged office girl, red lips, Bette Davis curls
A dance at the Floral Hall, Southport
Glenn Miller's Pennsylvania 6 5000
A midnight climb up a drainpipe
Nana finding a naked skinny lad on the landing
A surprise

Working Class Poem

This poem was born in a council house, rented flat, NHS hospital, caravan, servants' quarters, bed and breakfast, children's home, mortgaged house. This poem went to a state school and a university. This poem left school at 16. There are no whippets in this poem. This poem isn't going down a mine. This poem doesn't buy *The Sun*. This poem had free school dinners and uniform vouchers. This poem got into trouble. This poem went to night school. This poem had a social worker. This poem has no formal qualifications. This poem has a PhD. This poem was top of the class. This poem was a teenage parent. This poem is childless. Little is expected of this poem. This poem is framed on its parents' living room wall. This poem works as a university lecturer, shop assistant, hairdresser, teacher, call centre worker, filing clerk, police officer, bricklayer, food scientist, teacher, software consultant, sales person. This poem hasn't disclosed its occupation. This poem is unwaged. This poem likes films by Pasolini, Truffaut, Rohmer. This poem reads *The Beano*. This poem's father was a gas fitter. Its mother washed other people's floors. This poem watches live opera and ballet streamed to cinemas. This poem doesn't play football. This poem drinks beer, wine, spirits, tea, cappuccinos, is teetotal. This poem has never eaten mushy peas. This poem does not recognise itself in soap operas. This poem goes to art galleries, museums, poetry readings. This poem is an embarrassment. This poem goes to the pub. There is no tick box for this poem. This poem grew up on benefits. This poem pays higher rate tax. This poem isn't in an anthology. This poem doesn't have a glottal stop.

Confession

Bless me, unknown people on the internet, my hands are shaping quotation marks in the air when I say the word "sinned". Lies have been told on mortgage application forms; in hotel bars, bedrooms and churches; behind people's backs; in front of faces; at family dinner tables, job interviews; in rented premises used for business purposes; in court; in poems.

It's been many years. It's a matter of perspective.

I left the holiness of the poor behind; learned Home Counties vowels look attractive on job applications; went to Sloane Square in the Eighties, copied how they dressed. It brought the wages in.

Forgive me for the sin of making up my own identity; for not sitting easily inside a category; for leaving school with nothing; for learning languages from cassette tapes I borrowed from a public library; for liking literature and art and orchestras; for stuffing my face with a free university education before it ran out.

I'm far away from my council house. If I turned up there, they wouldn't know me.

And I'm not always kind to earnest people campaigning about class injustice. I've seen their childhood ski-ing holidays in their social media posts. They take the devil's shilling now, explaining that it funds good causes.

Forgive me for my prejudice.

I'm sorry for not confessing everything. Give me whatever penance you imagine I deserve. Only God knows if I say my prayers.

Then sometimes we'll think of Southport

How Napoleon liked the wide tree-lined avenues
and re-modelled Paris on it
and someone will say, no, Paris came first
and someone will say, no, *Southport* came first
and someone will talk about the faraway sea,
horses training on the sand, Red Rum,
Ginger McCain, our Dad riding all day,
too lazy to take the horse back to the stable
he gave it a slap
and someone will say
they didn't use the German name
because people didn't like *Germans,*
it was because he already *had* a family
in *Germany.* And someone will remember
Nana's biscuit tin, the smell of damp,
the softness of the biscuits,
our mother telling us not to eat them
and someone will say
he never had a riding lesson in his life
and someone will say you can't go to Paris
without thinking of Southport.

Dreaming while bereaved

Those dreams were almost visits to the cinema;
an exit place appeared; disappeared;

simultaneously I was actor and audience.
My mother died, then I dreamt of other people dying –

my father, two sisters, four brothers. I never knew
which night the roaming cinema of grief would visit.

The ones I loved the most had several showings.
The soundtrack was the sound I make when crying.

I dreamt for twenty years. Sometimes I was alone,
sometimes in a darkened room of almost silent people.

Sometimes I think about Red Rum

Yes, I remember that scene in *Terms of Endearment*,
after their mother's funeral, the children
at their grandmother's house, their new home,
little men in business-suits, the girl in a party dress.

The oldest boy is talking to Jack Nicholson,
a retired astronaut who lives next door,
says something like "But I can't swim there *now*, can I?"
gesturing towards the astronaut's swimming pool,

towards the grief of his own clothes.
Jack Nicholson says "Sure, you can,"
and the film ends, the children playing in sunlit water,
their bodies cleansed of their mother's illness.

Has it stayed with me because our mother also died?
although she was nothing like Debra Winger
and Southport isn't Texas. It was one of my uncles
who suggested the homecoming parade

after the packed church, faces turning towards us
as we followed behind the coffin, our confusion
when the gravedigger offered us his spade of soil,
our house crowded with people, no tea-cups left.

Red Rum's stable was behind Ginger McCain's
used car showroom. Paraded through Birkdale Village
the horse threw his head. People pushed forward
to touch him for luck. He wasn't red at all.

"But I can't shout hurray, *now*, can I?"
I would've asked Jack Nicholson, if he'd been there.

Indian Summer, 1980

In those days, for little money and bed and board,
you could employ a girl for housework and the children.
It's how we got our business started.
                              Mum died. Things fell apart.
                              I left school with hardly anything.

              Daylight was the colour of
stewed tea

                                        bad make-up
              impossible, you say,
        but look at the baby hanging there
            the leaves refusing to fall
                              what was his name?
what was her name?
that girl?

                                        the baby?
              who was always crying
              who never spoke?

              that Saturday in October
                    I took the baby to the swings
we dragged camping beds outside
the roses flowered again
              my summer of sleeveless charity shop dresses
                        raspberry lips, punky hair,
bloodshot eyes

              in the mornings
                        I wore a cardigan
                        spooned food in his mouth
kissed him goodbye

years later, I saw her in Pimlico
blond and smooth
as if someone had stroked her hair

           made it lie down

                        I had nowhere to live

I needed to work
                        I was used to babies
                            it was easy
I tried not to think of him

          he stood in his cot
        pushed the curtains aside
      watched me walk down the path
                  on Friday nights
                  the usual crowd

                  big house, they said
          my room up three flights of stairs
house prices were starting to rocket

        could have lost everything
if the market had turned
              they gave me a reference
                I got a job in Paris

              became someone else
we said the same thing
each time we got a new girl

        the gardens were parched
          the roses so pink
        headlines on the doormat

        how long will it last?

The domestic life of young film lovers

On Monday I blame Truffaut for my headache.
The 400 Blows always makes me cry.

On Tuesday we can't decide between Gene Kelly and Fred Astaire,
so end up watching both in different rooms.

Wednesday, Thursday, I plead fatigue – *Brief Encounter*
was on so late. By Friday the bed is shaking.

I fall asleep gazing at my bedside cabinet as if it's a window
in a jolting carriage. Sparsely-clad, and strangers,

we bump up against our marriage and roll away, as we journey through
the night, arriving, dishevelled, on Saturday morning with a lot to do.

In the queue at the supermarket, pretending to be *King Kong*,
you beat your chest and yell "A gorilla has his needs!"

It rains as we unload the car. We open biscuits, a coffee jar; read the list:
shopping/washing/cleaning. You vacuum with an erection. Singing.

Meanwhile rain shoots and spills from tiles and gutters, beating its tune
in time to thumping headboards. Slumped low in the afternoon,

we'll watch the geranium on our telly quiver and I'll catch your hand
as it falls against my breast, cage it inside my hand, kiss its fingers.

On Sunday when the lights go down,
with film magazines dead on the ground,

we talk about festivals we'd like to go to,
even though I can't quite hear you as you stand there,

ironing, staring into the distance, reminding me
of Celia Johnson, your head in a cloud of steam.

How to keep spare keys

Take nothing but one slice of bread
from the first house,
spread it with butter from the next,
dress in clothes shoved in plastic bags
curled up by bins. Your new life begins.

Sleep in attics.
Spy through cracks in doors,
scavenge down the backs of sofas,
when reading inscriptions
don't snap the spines of books.

Look at wedding gifts
stored in cupboards, drink leftover wine.
You'll see the tiny maps of gravy,
the wood lice, dried up,
where they keep the sharpened knives.

Slit no bridal gowns,
cut no throats, sell no babies
on the internet, feed pets.
Restlessness will take you
to jewellery stores and flower shops.

On ocean liners, in locked-up ballrooms,
save yourself the first waltz.
Moonbathe along deserted decks.
On scorching days
a butcher's meat safe provides relief.

In bitter weather
stroke discreet restaurant cats.
Find the names
of unborn children
on the backs of lost receipts.

Some of us understand
why our past plays out
in films and books;
need to look behind curtains
before we go to sleep;

keep quiet about our dreams:
the clarity of jam-jars left on windowsills,
the nudity of a hook, the feeling
we're being looked for, inside a rose bush,
in a tea caddy, under a stone.

A dream about Martin Scorsese

his era of extravagant eyebrows / a mustard-coloured wingback
chair / jaundiced gas fire / nicotine-stained at its centre / unlit /
my bedsit / Avenue Road / N6 / 1984 /

so / says Martin / manicured nails / cologne like toast burning /
you have a story? / jacket immaculate / cufflinks like jewels / there
is an idea I'd like to run by you /

so / so / so / a few more times / there's a woman / Martin punches
the air / jumps up / a woman! / yes / good beginning! / leaps to my
window / balloons out the nets /

who owns the car sounding its horn on the street? / I know where
I keep my notebooks / the many I will own through the years /
Martin is fighting his way out of yellowing nylon lace /

for the rest of my life / the feeling / the breath / the beginning

Our son the assassin

This morning we find him
rifling through the pockets
of dead people, stealing
jewellery and gold.

With a swirl of long robes
he conceals blades, scales
towers, lands inside hay bales,
pounds the streets with his hood up
while I blow on my tea.

"Mind those women!"
But he's already sent them flying,
plunged a knife
into three passing guards.

In our dressing gowns
we recall our resolve
never to buy him guns.
Aged 4, he bit a rice cake
into the shape of a pistol.

"Better he gets it out of his system now,
than when he's a grown man,"
says my husband, raising his voice
above the moans of the dying.

"Requiescat in Pace," mouths our son
and I imagine him
at my funeral;
scene from a black and white movie;
fistfuls of sand.

Telephony

I didn't know
I held the future
when I put seashells to my ear –
beach sand on my pillow
proof I'd heard seagulls crying.
Later, so much love from distant places
on trains, in cars, in restaurants,
and Alexander *must* have felt his heart skipping
when he spoke those words, *Come here, I want you.*
Yesterday, on the street,
a man spat *Bitch,*
imagining no-one in the world,
just her and him,
the phone so small,
he had to make a fist.

He had to make a fist,
the phone, so small,
just her and him
imagining no-one in the world.
A man spat *Bitch,*
yesterday on the street,
when he spoke those words, *Come here, I want you,*
and Alexander must have felt his heart skipping
on trains, in cars, in restaurants.
Later, so much love from distant places –
proof I'd heard: seagulls, crying;
beachsand on my pillow
when I put seashells to my ear.
I held the future.
I didn't know.

One on almost every street

The door to the red phonebox
on Liverpool Road
is heavy with importance
and we are precious
once inside.

The room is hushed
a tiny reference library
until the panther-black receiver
is placed against my ear
and I hear the purring
of an enormous cat.

Aged four, I'm small enough
to sit on the silver shelf
above the encyclopaedia-sized directories
while my sister, home from College,
phones her friends.

Cigarettes and bubble gum.
The man outside has stopped
frowning at his watch
and is staring in at us
as if we are unusual things
inside a fishtank.

Like the back of my hand

It takes me dream hours
        to cycle from our house
        in Leybourne Avenue
        to the lamppost
        on the corner of Raneleigh Drive

a handful of yards
        each gritty square of pavement
        cycled around intensively
        the sensation of toppling
        no knowledge of brakes

light from the faraway sea
        caught inside
        each small-windowed house
        as if I'm standing over myself
        as I dream

and only today
        a small birthmark on my wrist
        I've never seen before

The Extraordinary Jubilee of Mercy

In the Year of Mercy, when Holy Doors are opened
I ask the person I've long forgiven to leave and not return.

I light a match at every fireplace, incinerate his belongings,
fill birdfeeders with his leftover scraps.

I wash my floors of bootmarks, sponge fingerprints from lightswitches,
sweep my house of neglected dust. I rinse away his skin cells.

From my forgiveness I make an impenetrable fence
to grow flowers against. And when he calls through my letterbox,

I tell him, kindly, this is a Jubilee of Indulgence
before I fetch my hammer and my nails.

"Police Say Sorry"

Found poem from a Google search term

I have to say
really
I am sorry
we have been unable
to provide Blair Peach's family
with the definitive answers
regarding the terrible circumstances
in which he met his death

Mr Lawrence
Mrs Lawrence
I wanted to say to you
that I am truly sorry
that we have let you down

I can only express my regrets
to the family
of Jean Charles de Menezes

I absolutely agree
that we should apologise
for undercover officers
using the identities
of dead children

I apologise unreservedly
for the use of excessive
and unlawful force
which caused
Mr Tomlinson's death

I feel terribly sorry
for the victims
and their families –
I have singularly failed
victims of child abuse
in Rotherham

I am sorry
that Cherry Groce was shot
and left paralysed

I'm so sorry
we ignored victims of
child abusers Saville and Jaconelli

I would like to record
my sincere apology
that on the evening
Mark Duggan
was fatally shot by a police officer
a member of our staff
wrongly led the media
to believe that he had fired
at police officers

I acknowledge
that these intimate sexual relationships
by undercover officers
seeking to infiltrate protest groups
were a violation
of the women's human rights
and an abuse of police power

I unreservedly apologise

I'm sorry
we gave the letters addressed to them
telling them their daughters
were friends with a girl who'd gone to Syria
to their daughters and not to them
Clearly it's a terrible situation
I can only half-imagine
In that sense I am sorry

I unreservedly apologise

That day
96 people died
and the lives of many others
were changed forever

Today I want to apologise unreservedly

Many lessons were learned

It's almost impossible to imagine
how the same set of circumstances
could arise again

Stephen Lawrence isn't on the national curriculum

I tuck you in
with long ago and far away,
pull the blanket of *it wasn't us, it wasn't here*
around your heart, although I know
that five inches is 13 centimetres,
that 130 yards would cost a lot
of blood. There'll be Rosa Parks
and Martin Luther King for homework,
and someone saying it's good
we teach them that,
but no-one has a map of South-East London,
and today your teacher didn't say his name.
I teach you this: He spelled it with a 'PH'
not a 'V'. In 1993
he was eighteen.
He wanted to be an architect.
He was waiting for a bus.

Reading Harry Potter to my daughter

Impatient that the train to Hogwart's
isn't travelling fast enough,
she takes the book away,
leaves me so she won't miss
her appointment with the sorting hat.

Grateful, I sink into pillows,
daydream about holidays at the Granger's house,
the exhaustion of being different.

One more hour, I say
and she turns at my voice,
as if there are ghosts behind my shoulders,
as if I'm someone she's never met
and she's asking *Can you be trusted?*

In Privet Drive

The night before my eleventh birthday
their malice begins to tumble off me

like an unheld baby, as if I am no longer small
and shoved into a cupboard, as if my unhappiness

is a spell for vanishing. In my windowless room
I hear the owls calling me to grow beyond the chaos

of my childhood, to know that adulthood holds the keys
to magic. The sky is white with letters of acceptance,

my name is written. There's a giant coming
with a birthday cake. A trick for hiding scars.

Obliviate

A dash of mascara on my bedsheets
the only keepsake of my tears.
Once, I booked a dentist's appointment
to hear your voice again,
to feel Mum's rubbered finger in my mouth
gaze up at her
through the goggles. But I adjusted
to a new reality. I read Sartre:
We only become what we are
by the radical refusual
of that which others have made us.
Now, I can scarcely believe
we were related at all.

Winter in the town of three smells

Polish is spoken here
and mountains have appeared
behind the closed down meat-pie factory.
Bears roll their snouts like drunks,
lumber down, lick sticky locked-up gates,
dots of gristle stuck in rusted padlocks.

All of us, bears, wolves, humans,
raise our heads on windswept days,
inhale traces of bubbling hearts,
intestines, ears, blood.
Where there was once a brewery
there is now a flood of frozen weather.

They're playing violins around the edges,
frying herrings, the smell of beer rising
as skating couples bite into the ice.
Someone has bought clippers
to shave young men's heads
in kitchens, drinking black Economy tea.

Here is number for room,
for work in nice, clean-smelling factory.
Outside the Catholic Church, old women stamp snow,
wear fur at their throats, dab holy water like cologne.

After Christmas, we'll open our windows,
fill our houses with tripe and sweetened cabbages.
New Year will drift in
from the sewage treatment works.

Psychologies of Economy Ham

Because £1.10 buys 20 slices. Because one pack will make a loaf of sandwiches. Because it keeps all week. Because food is fuel. Because it costs my conscience £1.10 to put something into the Food Bank. Because I choose Premium Choice for myself but you will not know the difference. Because the label announces "Pack out a sandwich!" Because I was a wartime evacuee. Because there is something undeserving about a person who struggles to afford £1.10. Because we can fit 200 pigs in here. Because it's my turn on the Church Soup and Sandwich Run for the Needy. Because a government minister said he could live on £53 a week. Because anything else would be wasted on children. Because it is what I can afford. Because it is better than they would get in their own country. Because I am not fussy. Because I don't like waste. Because no-one showed me love so I have none to give you. Because I was given everything I wanted and do not believe anyone else is as important as I am. Because I expect you to eat something I wouldn't eat myself. Because I come from the same background and I have done alright. Because beggars can't be choosers. Because I lift food to my mouth before I die. Because one slice provides 11 calories, 0.3g of salt and 2.2g of protein.

Torrential

after Paul Stephenson's 'Deathflake'

I lie awake listening to the suicide, thinking about rain.
In the morning, a puddle of suicide on the floor.

"Can you come in early? The Head wants to talk about the rain."
I put on my suicide-proof coat and go out.

The sky is full of suicide. There's suicide rolling in from the hills.
"For some people, rain is taboo. They won't use the word."

Our coats are dripping with suicide. "Rain runs in some families."
We're all working out how to get home before the suicide comes.

"Don't glamourise rain. Don't talk about successful rain.
In the event of suicide, sports day will be cancelled."

That night there's hardly any suicide.
There's so much rain here. I feel it in my bones.

Meeting Ibaa

We chase
your daughter's blown away
painting, shouting key episodes
from our lives to each other
as if we're drowning.

From then on
when the bell rings,
we shine signals of friendship
over the rough sea of the playground

until it's time
to slump outside the school hall
waiting for the final thump
of the End of Year Disco.

You ask for my number –
People see this hijab
and look the other way.
We rummage for our phones

as if our bags are full of answers.
We spell out our names
and promise to meet again
but never do.

Poem in which we hear the word 'drone'.

You say drone
   and I think of bagpipes
      refrigerators
         aeroplanes
            I think of bees
          a male bee in a colony of bees
   which does no work
but can fertilise the queen
      the news left on, nobody listening
         at a party I was cornered in a kitchen
            by someone saying teacher, engineer, doctor
         someone saying terrorist
      the radio is saying people
at a market, buying flour and diesel
      coming home for lunch on a mountain path
         steady, deep humming
            an indolent person, an idler
         pass *away*, drag *out* (life, time)
      someone said bagpipes, someone said bees
a table, soup trembling, windowpanes spilling
      a pilotless missile
         directed by remote control

            one continuous note

              a low moan

Exquisite Corpse

In the writing workshop
I give my *shelf for a spinster* to Elinor.
She hands me *a clucking chicken.*
I have no-one to blame but myself
for *spilling soup* on the first line,
now *salted, stirred, heated, spiced*
and given back, with the chicken added.

She's made it alive,
added sound to food
that was feeding no-one,
but I'd wanted to write about life
before an explosion, an air attack –
life around a kitchen table –
holding spoons instead of pens.

It was Hilda's *nightdress*
made me think of a husbandless woman,
left on a shelf, but perhaps Elinor is imagining
thread, needles, woven cloth.

Whose daughter will telephone
first to say she didn't make it?
Which one of us will lie for days, unnoticed?
Who will be blown into a million pieces?

Three Ted Hughes Stories

My Ted Hughes story
is that he came to our school
and when he was elbow-deep
in a cow's womb, the calf's mooing head
hanging from the *mother's purpled elastic,*
he invited us to slide our hands *into the hot tunnel*
and a boy at the front fainted.

Mine is that I met him at Totleigh Barton,
said I was sorry I hadn't read him much
but that I'd never forgotten
the crow's *dark deadly eye,*
the *bounce and stab* of its beak.
He said, not in a mean way,
"It was a thrush."

My mother told me
our house would be *far out at sea all night.*
I touched her closed eyes,
her remembering face,
while the poem lowed in the dark
and we felt *the roots of the house move,*
the window tremble to come in.

Struggle, Thrushes, Wind

Daydreaming on a beach in Brittany

spilled purple on the cliffs like wine
      and green as if peppermint chews
           have melted down a gas fire

white person pink light, full as a teardrop
      two children making sandcastles
           a tremulous sky

I wouldn't be surprised
      if Eric Rohmer fell on my towel
           to explain the inevitability

of going home, in our peripheral vision
      a girl spading ribbons of ciné film
           from rock pools

a boy, blurred like Camembert
      straddling a moat

Speaking French

At the beach bar a man, half my age, is *centimètres*
from my sanded breasts, as beautiful as the *café crème*
between us, and what I still call *centimes*
lie blurred and glittered on my upturned palm.
"I am not my pair of glasses," I confide.

What have I learned since a driver shouted
down his bus that I had asked him for a ticket
to "The War"? That I would rather mime
my girlfriend's diarrhoea than be the man
standing in a crowded *pharmacie* chanting
"English, English," as if these syllables
are all it takes to halt ridicule
and stomach ache.

Poem in which I am Joséphine in Paris

after Rebecca Goss

Catherine Deneuve throws me the keys to her Rive Gauche
apartment, kisses the air above both of my ears.
I'm wearing her heels, shift dress, silk-lined coat.

My lipstick in place from my 7am café noir
to my 7pm coupe de champagne.
My hair has a just-left-the-salon gleam.

At parties, no-one pretends to be an emperor or jokes
that tonight's not the night. No one calls me 'Jo',
as if one syllable is all I deserve.

At outdoor cafés, waiters bring me tray after tray
of blossom-filled boulevards. The River Seine
lights up our faces. We're always on a film set.

When my husband calls my name
I hear the sound of a figure skater turning,
a delicious froth of consonants. Joséphine.

On every street corner, we stop to kiss.

Fallen asleep by a Christmas Tree
on New Year's Eve

When the singing in the street has stopped
I dream the year in fields.
Cowbells tip as baubles drop,
each hoof returns me to a kissing gate.

I tramp through fields of years,
my footprints waiting in the mud,
each thud returns me to a kissing gate
and trees are dragged from fields to streets.

My heart is slipping in the mud,
my dream is later than the last bus home,
there are dying trees in every street
and lovers sleep in moon-bright rooms.

The streets are later than the last bus home.
Fireworks glittered past our windows
though babies slept, lit up by moons,
untroubled by love or kissing gates.

Years have glittered past my windows,
now town clocks chime as baubles drop.
I snagged my heart on a kissing gate.
The singing in my house has stopped.

Ramshackle wooden structure
in the far, far distance

Obscured by wild orchards, seemingly remote but, nonetheless, within walking distance of a library, swimming pool and launderette – between stations I become the woman who lives there, who works part-time as a swimming instructor and lifeguard, who ensures her home is lined and insulated, on a raised base, to counter the possibility of mushrooms flourishing on internal walls.

My life is uncomplicated and uncluttered. I enjoy a satisfying friendship with the cook (there is a café at the pool). I bring him fallen apples and wild blackberries, he brings me wine and leftover Dish of the Day wrapped in foil. On mild evenings we sit outside on camping chairs, reminiscing about teatime television programmes and books.

I tell the children *It's you, not your parents, who'll know when it's time to deflate your buoyancy aids.* To the adult learners I say *Don't overanalyse your swimming dreams.* I know how to save a person's life.

When it's nearly dark I listen for the distant hoot of trains, look far beyond the trees for the glint of a passing carriage, see a woman reaching for her luggage, buttoning her coat. A sparsely-lit platform, fogged-up cars. She climbs inside, greets him with a kiss. I can't hear what they're saying of course. The taste of chlorine surprises him.

Old Girls

In the library, we lost ourselves
gazing at traffic, yearning
for stories of adventure and flight.

Now, every night,
we fly and hum,
our bodies carrying
the pollen of our lives –
dust from cinema seats,
grains of instant soup,
flakes of lubricating jelly.

Our headlamp eyes
unanchor rooms, turn
houses into ocean liners.
I've heard that children
born near motorways
can't sleep without the lullaby
of rolling tyres.

What becomes of the absent-minded?

our houses smell of burned apples
and pine forests   dripping through ceilings
we carry sausages   from room
to room   with a feeling
that someone wrote a song about us
we light ovens   cook emptiness
rooms become gummy   raw meat sweats
we remember the sausages   we remember the ovens
we forget how to spell 'margarine' and look at a block
on a plate   cut in half   fridge deep as a fjord
we remember   we are not Nordic translators
 in case we've met   we wave

Falling in love while watching *The Godfather*

Sonny Corleone didn't die at Jones Beach Causeway
        didn't lie beneath a sheet on Bonasera's table
                Don Corleone didn't say
                        Look, how they massacred my boy

On dead-end days in the Seventies
        he dodged the sparkling bullets
                to rescue me from Mrs Fletcher
                        writing equations on the board
he roared me down the road
        in a scream of open-topped chrome
                one manicured hand spinning circles
                        the other lazing against my nape

School desks swelled to tables under lemon trees
        the band played in the sun
                I wanted the weight of a gun in my hand
                I wanted to stand with the men

and Mrs Fletcher paused to sniff her fingers
        floured with chalk, and afternoons were flightpaths
                of particles of dust, and I wanted to be more
                        than Lucy Mancini as she shook against a door

Thanks for not switching me off

I'll have no concept of time
so, no rush, and I may fail to respond
normally to painful stimuli,
and to sound, but don't let that stop you
from playing me The Three Degrees
singing *When Will I See You Again?*
because even though I may be oblivious
to the doctor tipping light in my eyes
from her sterilised torch,
that doesn't mean I won't see again
Miss Travis,
Miss FitzSimons
and Mrs Cuthbertson,
or rather, three sixth-form girls
done up as them on the stage,
in gabardine raincoats, sturdy shoes,
clear plastic rain bonnets,
doing the moves, singing
hooo_ooh, haar_aarr,
precious mo_ments!

and wheeled to the daylight
I'll shake again,
a laughing girl again
in a sea of other laughing girls,
when the future flung open
the world's windows
and our lives soared in.
I'll fly again with oxygen in my blood –
the first time I'd understood love
when I dared to look at the three of them
on the day of their retirement.

They laughed too,
their rock-hard curls trembling,
tears bright
in their bat-wing glasses.
We never knew
if they liked the carriage clocks,
if they ever set
their hearts ticking.

History Lesson

I remember the fear of forgetting
the Austro-Hungarian Empire
under the cuffs of my school blouse.

Archduke Franz Ferdinand
and Sophie, his pregnant wife, are hiding
in my pencil case. The Black Hand,

Bosnia-Herzegovina and Serbia
aren't visible until I creep
my skirt three inches up my thigh

and Sarajevo, 28 June
1914 is folded so small
it's a blister on the sole of my foot.

I take Gavrilo Princip to my lips;
I would rather swallow ink
than hand him over.

Gavrilo

Friday afternoon, 1977. For 5B, the end of WWI
    can't come soon enough. *There is no need*
        to carry me to another prison, nail me
           to a cross and burn me alive.

Rachel, Julie, Amanda, Lesley R, Alison and Maria
    have paid Maria's brother to buy cider. As soon as
        the bell goes, they're meeting by the river.
           They'll get changed in the back of his car.

Once her folks have left, the party's at Amanda's.
    I am the son of peasants
        and I know what is happening
           in the villages.

Christine, Susan, Sally and Marian have agreed
    they'll finish their homework in the library,
        catch the 5 o'clock bus, get ready at Christine's.
        They have tickets for Star Wars.

Sarah D, Nicola D, Nicola C and Lesley G
    have closed their books. The other school's coach
        is on the drive. Lesley G (captain)
           is sending tactics under the table.

That is why I took revenge. I regret nothing.
    Dawn, Karen and Heather pause in their notetaking,
        mime pain, shake out their hands.
        They pity the popular set.

I am a Yugoslav Nationalist,
　　　　aiming for the unification of all Yugoslavs.
　　　　　　I do not care what form of state,
　　　　　　　　but it must be freed from Austria.

"He died on 28 April, 1918.
　　　　He weighed about forty kilos, six stone four.
　　　　　　His body wrecked by tuberculosis that ate his bones.
　　　　　　　　His right arm had to be amputated."

Unremembered girls somewhere in the room.
　　　　"His motives were revenge and love.
　　　　　　His legacy is ambiguous, to some a terrorist,
　　　　　　　　to some a national hero."

Drawing hearts and flowers around his name.
　　　　Not picked for netball teams
　　　　　　or parties or cinema trips.
　　　　　　　　His tiny frame beautiful, unthreatening.

In a room of large-scale charcoal self-portraits by Anita Taylor

I find you in this room of no apologising.
You refuse to sit up straight but show me
how you fail and try and fail again;
your hair a mess of lines and space,
you're smudged with the shadow of a face
you wore when you were younger.

In the beginning, charcoal crackled
across white paper; dust and sparks;
months of climbing ladders;
stepping back to understand.
If I leave you, there is no promise
that you'll stay the same.

In town for a funeral, we drive past our old house and see it is for sale

so we three sisters stumble home and find a widow
wandering from room to room, with a fragile smile,
as if she knows there's someone missing from our tale.

As we trail graveyard gravel along her doormat
she tells us hers: *We moved here to be near the sea
but within a year, he'd died.* We say we're sorry

and do not glide across the hallway ice-rink
the way we used to, or lasso our scarves
around the banisters, but we slide our dusty shoes

in spirals of our past and, when her back is turned, twirl
arthritic fingers over stories in the walls, lingering in
tiny swirls of punctuation, familiar under years of paint.

> On the news, balaclava'd, black-clothed men
> are abseiling again, down white stucco walls,
> exploding grenades, marking thirty years since
>
> the SAS raid on the Iranian Embassy at Prince's Gate.
> The smoke clears and I'm standing on the balcony
> held captive by the chaos, dogs barking
>
> like it's Bonfire Night, scenting death;
> shouting, screaming,
> men shot diagonally across their chests.

The cupboards, my sister mouths, shaping them
with her elegant hands, the alcove now
as bare as a face with its features blown out;

through the window the lilac tree still stands,
the rest of our garden tidied away;
coal shed; concertina doors – no fathoming

what serenely waits to be reclaimed,
the associations that we make across continents
and years; balaclavas our mother knitted

to protect our ears from seaside winds;
long boxes of Iranian dates at Christmas;
black clothes for funerals and raids.

The bathroom's small, the widow says,
as we huddle close
to where our family tidemark

has been rubbed away
and listen to each other breathing,
the gush of the boiler's blood.

When the hostages saw them,
sat on the ground with their hands
on their heads, their weapons thrown down,

saw them shot anyway,
they stood between the SAS
and the remaining terrorist.

Our mother died here, I want to say,
in our dreams she's trapped here still.
We form a quiet procession down the stairs,

following behind her, mourners in reverse,
gathering the strange logic of dreams,
strewn along the route to our front door.

A son will pull the trigger. Some nights he won't.
The widow will spread his winter coat
like a blanket on the beach and wait for him

to reach her. Sometimes he'll telephone from the
television to say he can't. A daughter will unravel
her long, black scarf, lasso it to the balcony,

a sister will storm the burning Regency room.
A lover will catch the bullets, resuscitate the one
who was thrown outside. Men with blown-off faces

will glide along this hallway, wearing balaclavas
on their feet instead of skates, not minding
they've had to wait for thirty years for one kind thought,

our mother leading them towards the open door.

The summer after Tamir Rice died

That night, our sons shaved their blond faces,
stank of cologne, dressed in suits, dined at long tables,
danced, celebrated finishing twelve years of school.

We waited for them at my house, deep in the garden.
Daylight still swirled in our wine glasses at ten,
the year's tipping point hung by the shining white roses.

The garden rang with a boyhood of summers;
their feet pounding the grass, their shouts and cheers.
The dark of the night rose around us,

our voices like a game of throw and catch,
his name in a place where boys lived,
older than twelve. We knew the truth of our sons,

tall for their age, who carried their laughing mothers
across kitchens, who looked and sounded like men
even as we kissed them in their pyjamas.

The others said they'd had similar thoughts,
except for June, who said she'd never heard of him.
Then there was hollering and our sons came lolloping

down the path, tripping over the rest of their lives,
as if the white roses had stepped out of their beds,
running, running towards us.

Love in the time of hospital visits

for Andrew

The first, I think, was my ankle, bandaged
as if the nurse was wrapping flowers
after it bloomed shamelessly
when I'd leaped from a style on College Lane
and danced in the Union Bar.

Next, your face.
A rugby boot tore it open
like a love letter
and a doctor sealed it,
not with a kiss, but with stitches.

Who needs fireworks
with an appendix like yours
bursting into our relationship?
Secretly, I was relieved I hadn't,
after all, poisoned you with my salmon.

You came to find me
when snow white linen
turned redder than a dozen roses.
Luckily, hospitals are equipped
to deal with all human spillages.

We've done our share of mopping.
Together, we've seen embryos
swimming past us on a screen;
one of them seemed to wave
as if to say she'd be our daughter soon.

(She kept her word).
Another time
we learned by ultrasound
we had a son
when he rudely somersaulted.

In 24 years, we've lost count
of all the body parts we've seen;
lost most of our inhibitions;
lost blood, skin, bone, joints,
teeth, hair, and dignity;

taken surreptitious snapshots
of each other wearing long white stockings.
And each time, it seems to me,
there have always been wheatfields,
artfully photographed, swaying,

and whales in black and white images
spraying air down airless corridors;
endless miles of linoleum;
perfume of boiled rice;
base note of disinfectant.

And in 24 years the smokers
wearing lace-ups with their dressing gowns
still haven't finished their cigarettes
or moved from the wooden bench
parked behind the ambulances.

We have seen each other
going under and coming round.
My love for you is as sound
as the money we've invested
in hospital car parks.

Even without your appendix
or your real knees; your shoulder, groin,
Achilles tendon, face, all re-arranged;
your ears re-attached; your prostate
gone missing;

you're someone I can rely on
to bring me gladness,
sometimes in a disposable cup.

Acknowledgements and Thanks

Acknowledgements are due to the editors of the following journals in which some of these poems, or versions of them, have previously appeared: *Butcher's Dog, Ink, Sweat & Tears, The Manchester Review, New Walk, The North, Poetry Wales, The Rialto, Under the Radar*. Several poems were previously published in the pamphlet *The Misplaced House* (tall-lighthouse 2014). i.m. Gareth Lewis. 'The Domestic Life of Young Film Lovers' won the Buzzwords Poetry Competition, 2017.

'Three Ted Hughes Stories' contains lines quoted in italics from poems by Ted Hughes: 'Struggle', 'Thrushes' and 'Wind'. 'Gavrilo' contains found material (in italics) from Wikipedia.

I would like thank the following people whose guidance and encouragement, in workshops or by correspondence or friendship, helped me to start writing again after a gap of ten years: The Aldeburgh Eight 2015, Jo Bell, Andrea Brady, Geraldine Clarkson, Rishi Dastidar, Sasha Dugdale, Helen Eastman and the Live Canon Ensemble, Carrie Etter, Rebecca Goss, Tania Hershman, Michael Laskey, Kathryn Maris, Helena Nelson, Stephen Payne, Pascale Petit, Isabel Rogers, Ann Sansom, Peter Sansom, Don Share, Hilda Sheehan, Richard Skinner, George Szirtes, Maria Taylor, Jackie Wills and Anthony Wilson.

Thank you to Anita Taylor and Gary Sangster at Drawing Projects UK, Trowbridge, for supporting poetry. Love and thanks to everyone in Trowbridge Stanza.

An enormous thank you to Jane Commane for guiding this book into being.

Finally, love and thanks to my many relatives whose ongoing encouragement and anecdotes feed my work: Cecily Corcoran; my cousins and their families; my siblings, their children and grandchildren; and my immediate family, Andrew, Kitty and Johnny Horsfall, whose unconditional love enables me to write. *These are the days.*